20TH CENTURY SCIENCE & TECHNOLOGY

1900-20

SHRINKING WORLD

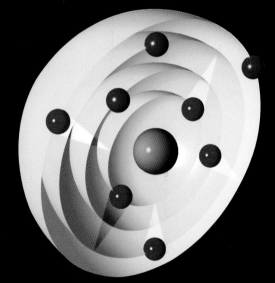

Steve Parker

Heinemann
LIBRARY

CONTENTS

At the dawn of the 20th century the only craft in the skies were a few balloons and airships. Within 20 years John Alcock and Arthur Brown had flown across the Atlantic Ocean, although they had a bumpy landing!

World War I was the first major conflict using engine power and motorized vehicles rather than just people and horses.

THE SCIENTIFIC CENTURY

In our modern world of the Internet, mobile phones, routine satellite launches and daily heart transplants, it is difficult to imagine life just one hundred years ago. There was no radio or television. No aircraft, washing machines or antibiotic drugs. Only a few rich and important people had cars or electricity in their homes. But the first two decades of the 20th century saw enormous changes in daily life – due mainly to the progress of science and technology.

The science of electronics leaped ahead in 1907 with the triode vacuum radio tube or 'valve'. Soon they were in mass production.

In particular, one major invention brought huge changes. This was the factory with its assembly lines and mass production methods. Factories started to churn out millions of new products. Prices for goods fell. Soon all kinds of machines and gadgets found their way into ordinary people's lives. Sadly the idea that a big military conflict speeds scientific progress came true with the horrors of World War I (1914–18). But by 1920 a more peaceful, more prosperous and more scientific era had arrived.

Photography was only for wealthy experts, until the Kodak company introduced the 'Brownie' easy-to-use snapshot camera in 1900.

BIG IDEAS

Some of the biggest scientific ideas of 1900–20 involved the smallest parts of the Universe – atoms. At least, that is what scientists thought. But as they experimented using new high-power electrical equipment, it became clear that atoms were not the smallest particles. What were they made of?

INSIDE THE ATOM

By about 1910 scientists realized that atoms were made of even tinier particles. There seemed to be three types. Protons had positive electrical charge, electrons had negative charge and neutrons had no charge. But how were they arranged in an atom? There were many theories and arguments.

— Positive nucleus (contains protons and neutrons)

Electron shell

Negative electrons

THE RAISIN PUDDING ATOM

Around 1900 one of the main ideas for the structure of the atom was the 'raisin pudding theory' of Joseph John Thomson (1856-1940). He had discovered electrons in 1897. He suggested that an atom was a general area or atmosphere of positive charge with electrons scattered in it – like raisins mixed in a pudding.

Atmosphere of positive charge

Electron

Ernest Rutherford suggested that the protons and neutrons were gathered together in a central area, the nucleus. Electrons whizzed around the nucleus like planets in orbit around the Sun. Neils Bohr said that electrons usually stayed at certain distances from the nucleus, moving in regions called 'shells' but sometimes jumping from one shell to another. This is the idea we use today.

Electrons jump shells

Ernest Rutherford (1871–1937) was born in New Zealand and did his main research in England. In 1911 he was first to suggest that an atom had a dense central area, the nucleus. He also discovered the particle called the proton. In 1919 his team was first to split apart an atom.

Danish physicist Neils Bohr (1885-1962) said that electrons did not wander freely in an atom. They stayed at fixed distances from the nucleus. This was an early use of the scientific idea called quantum theory.

Since the late 1600s scientists had used the ideas of Isaac Newton to explain gravity, energy and how objects move – from atoms to planets. In 1905 Albert Einstein wrote a scientific article about 'special relativity' which changed this view for ever. He followed it with an article on general relativity in 1915. It says that almost nothing, not even time, is constant. Nearly everything is relative, in particular depending on speed. As something moves faster, time passes slower. So if you go on a fast space journey for a year, when you come back, two years may have passed on Earth. Relativity also says that very strong gravity, such as near a star, can 'bend' space. So straight lines go in curves. The only constant quantity is the speed of light, 300,000 km/sec.

Einstein's theories of relativity were verified when light rays from a distant star were observed to bend as they passed close to the Sun.

7

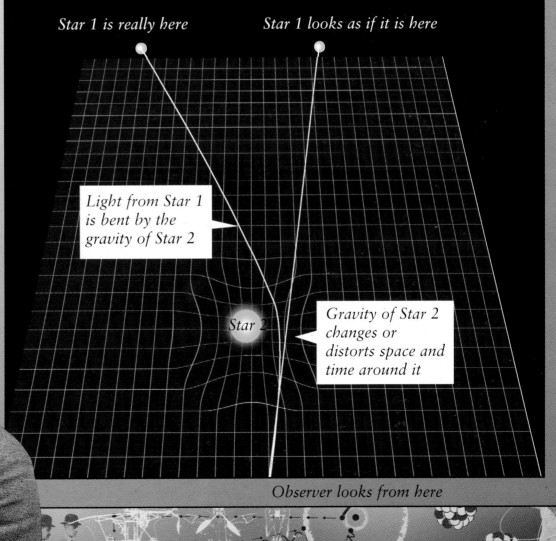

Star 1 is really here

Star 1 looks as if it is here

Light from Star 1 is bent by the gravity of Star 2

Star 2

Gravity of Star 2 changes or distorts space and time around it

Observer looks from here

WORLD SCIENCE

In previous centuries, wars were mainly a matter of planning and tactics, with people and guns. As World War I broke out in 1914, military experts realized they had several new types of machines and technologies to help them win. Suddenly scientific research speeded up enormously. Victory would come to the side with the best weapons of destruction.

Assembly lines for mass production were developed in 1913 for cars. They were soon adapted to make war equipment or munitions.

Tanks or 'landships' first saw action at the Battle of the Somme in 1916. Their caterpillar or crawler tracks could cross mud and trenches.

THE BATTLE ON LAND

A new type of land vehicle developed for war was the tank. Its crawler tracks were originally invented for tractors in muddy fields (see page 17). The tank was protected by a new type of very hard steel known as armour plating, and powered by the diesel engine which had been developed some 25 years before.

Submarines quickly became effective secret weapons at sea. Early military subs like this U15 (1914), being rammed by cruiser HMS Birmingham, *had diesel engines or electric motors.*

WAR AT SEA

By 1900 the age of sail was already slowly dying away. Sea vessels were driven by steam or diesel engines. But warfare demanded faster ships. A new type of propulsion was the steam turbine. High-pressure jets of steam blew against angled blades (like those of a fan) on a shaft and made it spin with great speed and power. Steam turbines had been in use since the 1880s in electricity power stations, to turn generators. They were quickly adapted for use in ships where the shaft spun the screw (propeller). In 1906 the battleship *Dreadnought* set a new trend, with a few large guns which could be tilted up or down, mounted in swivelling turrets.

THE FIRST WAR IN THE AIR

At the start of World War I aircraft were used for reconnaissance (spying or 'spotting' the enemy's positions) and carrying messages. Just four years later aerial warfare raged as fighter planes machine-gunned ground troops or each other and bombers dropped mass explosives on the enemy. All of these craft were powered by internal combustion (petrol-type) engines. But the pressure of warfare meant their speed and power increased hugely. The first plane-plane battle in October 1914 involved a Voison LA III with a top speed of 110 km/h. Three years later the SPAD XIII was smaller but went twice as fast. A great advance was the interrupter. It made the aircraft's machine gun fire directly forwards past the propeller without hitting it. Having the machine gun right next to the pilot meant it could be aimed much more accurately.

Fighter planes in a 'dog fight' in 1918.

POWERED FLIGHT

Before 1900 the only flying craft were balloons, which went where the wind blew them, and longer slimmer balloons with engines called airships. Within three years two new craft had taken off.

THE AIRSHIP ERA

German nobleman Ferdinand von Zeppelin (1838–1917) wanted people to travel long distances in luxury, as on an ocean liner, but in the sky. In 1900 he launched the first rigid airship or dirigible. It had a metal frame and bags of lighter-than-air hydrogen gas to stay aloft. Soon airships were carrying passengers over the oceans.

The Wright brothers, Wilbur (1867–1912, right) and Orville (1871–1948), and their first plane, called the Flyer.

THE FIRST PLANE

In 1900 about ten teams of inventors and scientists were trying to make the first powered, controllable, heavier-than-air flying machine – an aeroplane. Success came to two brothers who ran a bicycle business in Dayton, Ohio, US. From about 1890 Wilbur and Orville Wright had studied birds, kites and gliders to understand the science of flight. They made their own petrol engine since others of the time were too heavy. Their *Flyer* made its first 12–second trip at Kitty Hawk, North Carolina on 17 December, 1903.

THE FIRST EPIC FLIGHT

The first flight in Europe was not until 1906, three years after the Wrights' success. The first air show in 1909 near Reims, France attracted 38 craft. Only 23 managed to take off but the event marked aviation as a serious science and industry. In July of the same year Louis Blériot flew across the Channel from Calais, France to Dover, England in his *Blériot No XI* plane. He took 37 minutes to cover 37 kilometres, won a prize of £1,000 from the London Daily Mail newspaper, and became a world celebrity.

Blériot's craft was an early monoplane, with two wings instead of a biplane's four.

Large rigid airships became known as 'zeppelins' after their inventor. They were luxurious and faster than land or sea travel. But they were easily grounded or damaged by bad weather. There was also the risk that the very light hydrogen gas inside might catch fire.

HOW AIRCRAFT STAY UP

An aircraft stays in the air because of the shape of its wings. Seen from the side these are more curved on the upper side than on the lower side, a shape known as the aerofoil section. As the wing moves forwards air rushes over and under it. Because the upper surface is more curved, the air flowing over it moves faster than the air beneath. Faster airflow means lower air pressure. So the air pressure below the wing is higher than the air pressure above. The result is that the wing is pushed upwards by a force called lift. This keeps the plane up.

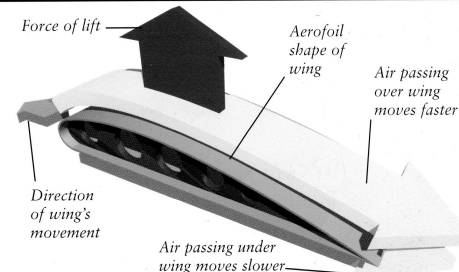

Force of lift

Aerofoil shape of wing

Air passing over wing moves faster

Direction of wing's movement

Air passing under wing moves slower

NEW TECH

Many technologies that we now use without thinking every day, especially waves for radio and television, were developed in the early 1900s.

RADIO

The idea of invisible waves passing through air at the speed of light was nonsense for most people in 1900. Italian engineer Guglielmo Marconi had sent these so-called 'radio waves' over several kilometres. But few people could see how radio might be useful. In 1901 Marconi built a massive radio transmitter in Cornwall, England and succeeded in sending radio waves nearly 3,000 kilometres across the Atlantic to Newfoundland, North America. The world shrank as long-distance communication became almost instant. By 1915 people could talk on the telephone across the Atlantic Ocean.

GETTING THERE FASTER

The rise of the aeroplane had rapid effects on other forms of transport. In 1907 the first hydrofoil boats sped across the water, the hull lifted clear of the surface on the 'water skis' beneath. The skis had aerofoil shapes to produce an upward force just like an aircraft wing. Hydroplanes were flat-bottomed boats with aircraft-type propellers. They could travel across swamps and reedy waterways where an underwater propeller would become tangled in the weeds.

By about 1920 the airscrew-driven hydroplane was a new form of transport along plant-choked rivers such as the Amazon in South America and the Tigris in the Middle East.

MOVING PICTURES

Photography was already well established by 1900. Colour photos began in 1891. But these were all 'stills'. The first moving pictures were shown in Paris in 1895 by the Lumière brothers Auguste (1862–1954) and Louis (1864–1948). Soon their invention became a new form of entertainment, the cinema. In the early 1900s crowds flocked to watch the seemingly magical spectacle of people, scenes and events on the big screen. Movie cameras and projectors rapidly became larger and more powerful. Live shows with singers and dancers in local music halls began to suffer. Technology could bring world-famous film stars, songs and newsreels into every neighbourhood.

Guglielmo Marconi (1874–1937) carried out many tests on his radio equipment in the garden of his family home in Bologna, Italy, before coming to England in 1896.

STRANGE PLANES

After the Wright brothers made their first flight, inventors tried to build improved types of planes. One idea was that the more wings a craft had, the better it would fly. All kinds of weird machines were constructed, some with more than 50 small wings. But the Wrights' scientific wind tunnel tests showed that one wing too near another would disrupt the airflow over both, and so lessen their lifting force.

A 'multiplane' being tested in France, circa 1900.

THE PICTURE PROJECTOR

During the 1800s audiences paid to come into halls and watch 'lantern slides' – transparency images shone by a powerful light projector on to a large screen. There was no television and few people could afford photography, so the giant pictures were great entertainment. The movies or cinema meant new equipment like this Gaumont 1903 dual projector for still and moving images.

Film spool or reel

Projection lens

Lantern (lamp)

Electric motor to wind film spools

Electrical connections

ON THE ROAD

The first cars came on the roads in the 1890s. By 1900 they were being made in small factories, in hundreds each year. In 1903 a US industrialist founded a new auto company and motoring changed for ever. His name was Henry Ford (1863–1947).

'ANY COLOUR ...

... As long as it's black' was one of Ford's sayings. He wanted to mass produce cars so that ordinary people could afford them. In 1913 he set up a moving assembly line where workers added parts as the cars went past. This cut production time for a Model T from 12 to two hours.

Model T Fords or 'Tin Lizzies' were made from 1908. Ford's production methods were soon used around the world.

STEAM, ELECTRIC OR PETROL?

The first automobiles were not all petrol-powered. There were electric cars with batteries and also cars powered by steam engines. In the early 1900s they competed for the mass market. Early world speed records were held by the 'Stanley Steamer' and by several electric cars. But in 1913 a new method of producing petrol from crude oil was developed and petrol engines took over.

This Jenatzy electric automobile was the first car to go faster than 100 km/h, in 1899.

A petrol engine burns or combusts its fuel inside a chamber called the cylinder, so it is known as an internal combustion engine. In the first of four stages, a mix of fuel and air is sucked in (induction). The mixture is squashed hard by the piston (compression). A spark plug ignites it and the mini-explosion pushes the piston powerfully (combustion). The waste gases are then pushed out (exhaust).

Internal combustion engine cycle

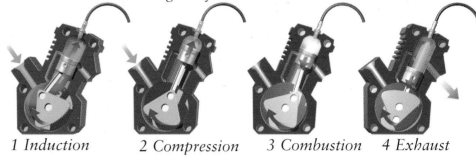

1 Induction   2 Compression   3 Combustion   4 Exhaust

PUBLIC TRANSPORT

Even by 1920 in regions such as North America and Europe, most people could still not afford to buy a car. However public transport had moved from the horse-drawn cart to the engine-driven omnibus. *Omni-* means 'all' could travel, although the name was soon shortened to 'bus'. Trams combined road and railway vehicles, with rails set into the roadway. As streets became more crowded the first traffic lights appeared in 1914.

London's first tram network opened in 1903. The carriages had electric motors and switched points for different routes just as on a railway.

Trips on motorized buses and coaches, like this 1919 outing to the seaside, became a new form of leisure activity. There were no horses to worry about and the vehicle could cope with heavy suitcases.

15

TRAVEL TIME

Motors and engines became more powerful and reliable. Vehicles and craft became safer and more comfortable. Soon long-distance transport began to take off. The first regular aircraft service began between Tampa and St Petersberg in Florida, USA on New Year's Day, 1914.

Passengers and mail board a London-Paris service in 1919. There was no cabin heating so they had to wrap up well against the cold air at high altitude.

THE FIRST AIR SERVICE

Planes were not the first flying craft to carry people on scheduled routes. The German DELAG company began airship passenger trips in 1909. It flew the first international flights from Germany to Sweden. But like the early passenger planes they were often grounded by breakdowns and bad weather.

The 'unsinkable' Titanic had watertight compartments which could be sealed separately, so flooding from damage in one place could be limited. But on its first voyage in April 1912 the ship hit an iceberg and sank with the loss of about 1,500 lives.

A VERY SHORT SHORT-CUT

Ocean travel was slow but more comfortable and reliable than by air. However a coast-to-coast journey in North America meant an enormous trip around South America. The Panama Canal across a narrow stretch of Central America cut this journey by 11,200 kilometres. After a false start in the 1880s the canal was begun again in 1904 and completed 10 years later. It was seen as a modern wonder of the world (see page 27).

The Panama Canal is 65 kilometres long and up to 90 metres wide. New types of concrete were used to build six pairs of locks, each 305 metres long and 34 metres wide. These raise the water level 26 metres.

16

DISASTER AT SEA

In 1904 Cunard's *Carmania* was the first ocean liner to be powered by steam turbines (see page 9). However disasters followed. *Titanic* sank in 1912, then the liner *Lusitania* was sunk by a German submarine in 1915 with the loss of about 1,200 lives. This attack helped to push the USA into World War I.

As a result of the *Titanic* tragedy, in 1915 French scientist Paul Langevin (1872–1946) devised sonar to detect icebergs, submarines and other dangers. Sonar or echo-sounding sends out 'pings' of sound waves which travel through water at 1,500 metres per second. They bounce back off objects as echoes and are detected by a hydrophone (underwater microphone). The direction and time delay of the echoes show the object's position and distance. Sonar means SOund NAvigation and Ranging. It is also used to map the seabed, locate sunken wrecks and find shoals of fish and other sea creatures.

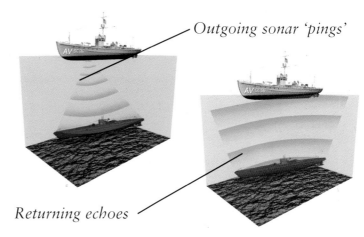

Outgoing sonar 'pings'

Returning echoes

This farm tractor from about 1905 had a new type of wheel propulsion called caterpillar or crawler tracks. But driving the heavy tracks used vast amounts of fuel so most tractors had ordinary tyres with deep tread (ridges).

ON THE MAKE

Electric motors and petrol or diesel engines were not only used in vehicles. They were installed in factories to power machinery for mass production. Coupled with many kinds of new materials and bigger, better assembly or production lines, factories were able to produce thousands of products every day for the new boom in consumer goods.

MATERIALS GALORE

As a result of pioneers such as inventor Thomas Edison (1847–1931) and car-maker Henry Ford, research changed greatly in the early 1900s. Instead of a talented but untrained amateur working alone in an attic, trying to have a bright idea, teams of scientists were set up to work on specific tasks in 'inventions factories'. This greatly helped progress in materials technology, especially developing new kinds of metals for building, vehicles and factory goods.

Assembly lines began with cars but the idea soon spread to making all kinds of products, from bottles to houses.

The Fuller Building in New York City was nicknamed the 'Flatiron Building' from its triangular shape like a smoothing iron. It was completed in 1903 and stood 21 storeys and 87 metres tall. It was one of the first tall buildings with a frame made of steel rather than wrought iron, possible due to a new process that produced 'rolled steel' beams.

NEW ALLOYS

Some of the busiest areas of research involved alloys – metals mixed with other substances. One of these new alloys was stainless steel, a combination of iron and carbon as in normal steel plus the metal chromium. Stainless steel is very resistant to wear and rusting. British scientist Harold Brearley (1871–1948) investigated its use for guns but by 1914 stainless steel knives were being made in Sheffield, England. Other steels were developed for buildings, especially for metal 'skeletons' in the new tall buildings known as skyscrapers.

Stainless steel was first developed as a possible metal for rifle barrels. But it was soon used for knives, forks, pans, sinks and other kitchen items.

THE BONES OF A BUILDING

Traditional buildings used walls as their main strength. These supported the floors and also the walls above. From the 1880s in Chicago, USA a new method took shape with metal beams and girders as the framework or 'skeleton'. Floors and walls were attached to this. In the early 1900s new steels and girder designs meant skyscrapers shot up. Tallest from 1914 to 1929 was the Woolworth Building in New York City, with 60 storeys standing 241 metres high.

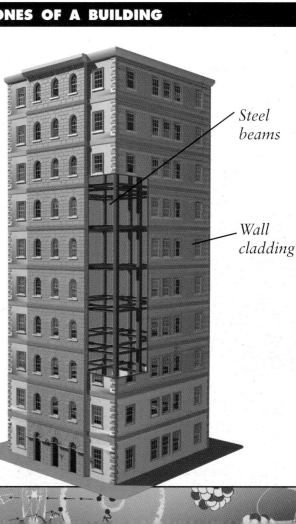

Steel beams

Wall cladding

START OF AN ERA

One of the most important resources in the world today is petroleum (crude oil). We use it to make petrol, diesel and other fuels, also lubricants, tars, asphalts, preservatives, plastics, paints, dyes and hundreds of other products. The petroleum industry increased rapidly from about 1910 with new methods to separate or 'crack' crude oil into its many component parts or ingredients.

Advances in manufacturing industry around 1900 saw a new type of glass called Pyrex. It could withstand the very high temperatures in ovens.

CHEMICAL FACTORIES

Increasing scientific research meant greater need for raw materials. Some of the most important were nitrogen-containing chemicals such as nitric acid. Nitrogen-rich fertilizers were also needed for farming. The Haber-Bosch process (below) meant faster, cheaper production of nitrogen chemicals – including explosives.

Petrol became much cheaper to make from about 1913.

A USEFUL PROCESS

German chemist Fritz Haber (1868–1934) was awarded the Nobel Prize for chemistry in 1918, for his part in developing the Haber-Bosch process. This took nitrogen gas (N_2), which makes up four-fifths of air, and combined it with hydrogen (H_2) to make ammonia (NH_3). Ammonia is one of the basic substances in the chemical industry. It is used to produce nitric and nitrous acids, cleansers, disinfectants, synthetic fibres, refrigeration fluids and artificial fertilizers.

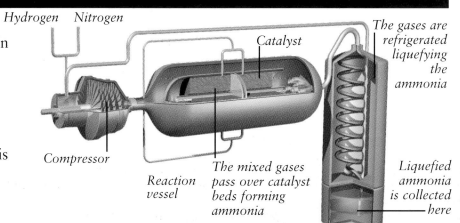

Hydrogen   Nitrogen

Catalyst

The gases are refrigerated liquefying the ammonia

Compressor

Reaction vessel

The mixed gases pass over catalyst beds forming ammonia

Liquefied ammonia is collected here

20

THE HIGH-TECH FARM

For thousands of years farming relied on animals such as horses and oxen to pull ploughs and their droppings to enrich or fertilize the soil. But engine-powered tractors could work longer hours and did not need care, stables or food. Also artificial fertilizer packed 1,000 times more nutrients into each small, light bag compared to animal dung. Agricultural science boomed.

A 'mechanical horse' tractor from 1917.

SAFER ELECTRICITY

The increasing use of electrical equipment meant the need for cases, handles and other parts made from insulators – materials which resisted the flow of electricity. Metals were little use since most are conductors, carrying electricity very well. This led to the invention of one of the first synthetic plastic-type materials, bakelite. It was made in 1909 by a Belgian-American chemist, Leo Baekeland (1863–1944).

→ Bottled gas and chemicals

THICK, DARK – AND WORTH A FORTUNE

→ Petrol (gasoline)

→ Chemicals
→ Jet fuel and kerosene
→ Diesel fuels and heating oils
→ Chemicals

→ Lubricating oils

→ Wax candles, polishes and chemicals
→ Fuels for ships, factories and central heating

→ Tars for roads and roofing

Crude oil

The first oil wells were drilled in Pennsylvania, USA in 1859. The main substance obtained from the thick, black crude oil was kerosene to burn in lamps. At first petrol (gasoline) from oil was a waste product. Then in the 1900s it was found to be an ideal fuel for engines. The oil industry boomed. Crude oil was heated to separate it into its many useful different parts or constituents.

By about 1910 the street lights in many big cities were being converted from gas to electricity.

ELEC-TECH

Electricity is our most useful and widespread form of energy, supplied to almost every home and building in developed countries. At the start of the century most people, even in big cities, did not have electricity. They used oil or gas lamps and burned coal and wood for heating and cooking. But soon the electricity wires began to arrive in offices, factories and homes.

In 1915 AT&T succeeded in making the first transatlantic transmission between Virginia, USA and the Eiffel Tower in Paris using radiotelephony. Radiotelephony is a way of communicating by radio waves instead of along a wire. The first proper radiotelephone was produced by US inventor R. A. Fessenden in 1900.

CONSUMER BOOM

From the beginning electricity was a clean, adaptable and popular form of power compared to smelly gas and sooty coal. A whole new range of electrical consumer equipment became available such as the electric typewriter (1901), vacuum cleaner (1901–2), washing machine (1908), toaster (1909) and refrigerator-freezer (1913). In 1917 Clarence Birdseye (1886–1956) devised a way to preserve food in a convenient way in freezers.

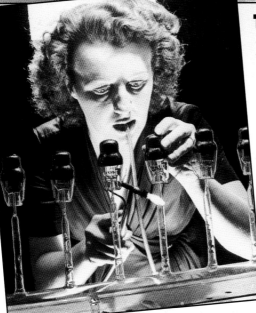

The triode (radio oscillator tube or amplifier vacuum tube) was nicknamed the 'valve' because it controlled the flow of electricity like a tap valve controls the flow of water. Valves made possible many new kinds of electrical equipment.

THE BEGINNING OF ELECTRONICS

In 1907 US inventor Lee De Forest (1873–1961) devised an electrical device called the triode. This worked as an amplifier, using small electrical currents to control much larger ones. It also made electricity reverse in direction, or oscillate, very quickly and powerfully which was ideal for producing radio signals. These advances allowed the first telephone calls across the Atlantic Ocean between Arlington, Virginia, US and Paris in 1915.

POWER FOR THE NATION

An electricity power station changes one form of energy, such as the heat from burning coal or oil or gas, into another form of energy, electricity. The heat boils water into high-pressure steam that blasts against the fan-like blades of a turbine, making them spin. The turbine shaft is linked to a generator that uses magnets and coils of wire to produce electricity.

Steam leaves turbine to condensers for cooling

High pressure steam enters turbine

Turbine shaft

Turbine

Generator

Turbine blades rotate at high speed

The electric cooker was one of the many new electrical appliances. Improved versions with hot plates and ovens date from about 1919.

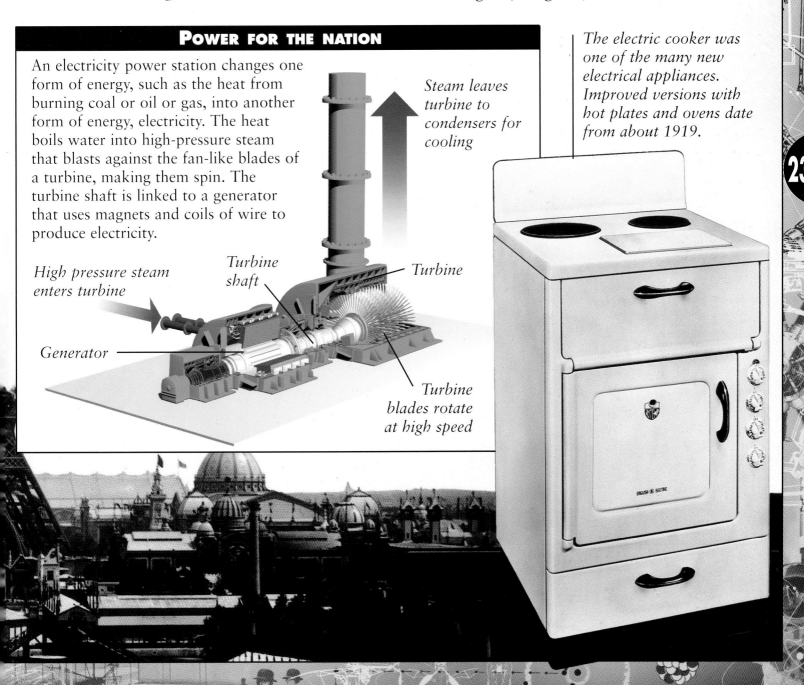

MEDICAL SCIENCE

In 1895 a chance discovery in a physics laboratory in Würzburg, Germany, changed medicine for ever. German scientist Wilhelm Roentgen discovered new and powerful rays. They were invisible and mysterious so he called them X-rays until they received a proper name. We still call them X-rays today.

AN ELECTRIC TUBE

Roentgen was experimenting with a vacuum tube, an electrical device with a glass container from which all air had been removed. Very powerful electricity was passed between two contacts or electrodes in the tube. In fact the vacuum tube was a simple forerunner of the valve, the cathode ray tube and, in the 1920s, the television set.

Within weeks of discovering X-rays, Roentgen was working with doctors on their medical uses.

GLOWING CRYSTALS

Roentgen noticed that a piece of paper coated with a certain chemical glowed whenever the vacuum tube was switched on. Even if he put a thin sheet of metal between the tube and the paper, the paper still glowed. He guessed that some type of powerful rays were passing through the metal.

Roentgen (1845–1923) received the very first Nobel Prize for physics, in 1901, for his discovery of X-rays.

USEFUL BUT HARMFUL

Less than three months after Roentgen's discovery X-rays were used to look for broken bones, swallowed objects, tumours (growths) and other problems inside the body. Before X-rays the body had to be cut open. However from 1902 X-rays came under suspicion. Some people exposed to them developed cancers and other health problems. In the 1950s scientific tests showed that large amounts of X-rays could harm. So they were used with more caution.

An early X-ray demonstration.

SEEING INTO THE BODY

Roentgen wondered if the rays could pass through the body. An X-ray photograph of his wife's hand showed that they went through muscles, blood and other soft parts, but not through bones. So X-rays became a marvellous way to see the skeleton inside a living person.

Mobile X-ray units in vans were used in World War I, to check injuries to troops near the battlefield.

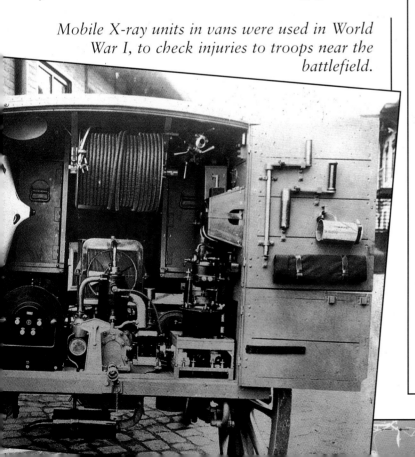

THE X-RAY MACHINE

X-rays are part of a range of waves and rays known as the electromagnetic spectrum, made of electrical and magnetic energy. Light rays, radio waves and microwaves are also in the spectrum. X-rays are made by firing bits of atoms called electrons (see page 6) at very high speed against a metal target plate. The very heavy, dense metal lead is used as shielding.

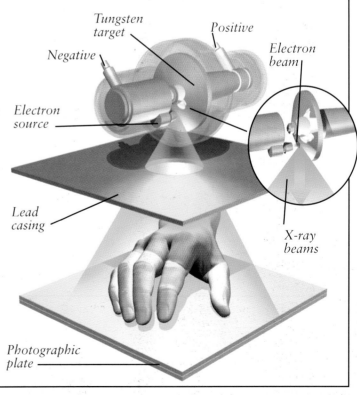

Tungsten target
Positive
Negative
Electron beam
Electron source
Lead casing
X-ray beams
Photographic plate

BLOOD AND GUTS

Blood transfusions involve putting blood, or parts of it, from one person into another. They are vital in modern medicine. People had tried transfusions for centuries, even using animal blood, but the patients nearly always died. In 1900 Karl Landsteiner decided to find out why.

MIXING BLOOD

Landsteiner carried out experiments with blood from himself and five colleagues in test tubes. In certain cases the samples mixed smoothly but in others they formed clot-like lumps. He tested the blood samples for different substances and worked out that there were four different kinds or groups of blood: A, B, AB and O. Only certain groups could mix safely. This made blood transfusions much safer.

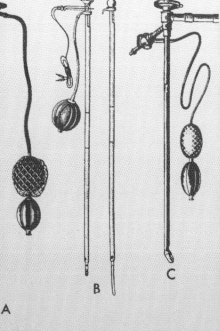

Austrian physician Karl Landsteiner (1868–1943) was awarded the Nobel Prize for medicine, or physiology, in 1930.

THE ABO BLOOD GROUP SYSTEM

There are four groups in the ABO blood group system. Only certain combinations can be mixed safely, as when a patient receives a transfusion. Group O is called the universal donor since it can be given to any person. Group AB is the universal recipient because it can mix with any other group. Usually doctors try to give a patient blood of the same group.

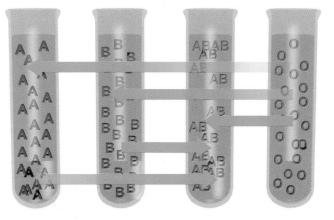

Green arrows indicate which blood groups can be safely mixed within the human body.

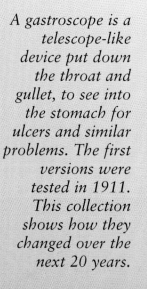

A gastroscope is a telescope-like device put down the throat and gullet, to see into the stomach for ulcers and similar problems. The first versions were tested in 1911. This collection shows how they changed over the next 20 years.

26

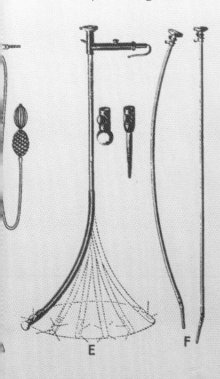

Larva (grub)   Male   Female

A DREADED FEVER

Yellow fever is a serious, often deadly disease of tropical places. In 1888 work on the Panama Canal was abandoned because hundreds of workers died from it every month (see page 16). In 1900 a team of US army doctors led by Walter Reed (1851–1902) began experiments in Havana, Cuba. People volunteered to be bitten by the suspected carriers of the disease – mosquitoes. The results showed that mosquitoes were indeed the carriers. After a great campaign to wipe out the insects, the disease was conquered in the area by 1906.

The mosquito that spreads yellow fever is Aëdes aegypti. Only the female carries the viruses (germs) – the adult male does not feed. The female bites a yellow fever sufferer, sucks up blood containing the germs, then bites someone else and so transfers the germs.

THE RIGHT TO HAVE BABIES

In the 1900s women campaigned more actively for equality with men, such as the right to vote. The campaigns spread to health and medicine. New York nurse Margaret Sanger invented the term 'birth control' in 1914, saying women should be able to choose to have sex but not get pregnant. English scientist Marie Stopes wrote a book *Wise Parenthood* (1920) to tell ordinary people the facts about sex and pregnancy.

27

E   F

Marie Stopes (1880–1958)   *Margaret Sanger (1879–1966)*

GADGETS

With more factories and more mass production, hundreds of new machines, gadgets and devices came on to the market every year. People began to buy new products instead of trying to mend old ones. The 'throwaway society' arrived in 1901 with the disposable razor blade.

SOUND SCIENCE

The phonograph for playing recorded sounds had been invented by Thomas Edison in 1877. In 1888 the German-US engineer Emile Berliner (1851–1929) improved its design. Instead of storing sounds as a

Foodmixers and blenders date from about 1910. They took the hard work out of stirring in the kitchen.

wiggly groove on a cylinder, he used a flat disc. In 1904 he made further improvements by making the discs from harder-wearing acetate materials so they lasted longer.

This gramophone dates from about 1891. By 1900 such devices were being fitted with electric motors, and by 1910 with electronic valve circuits and loudspeakers.

US inventor King Gillette dreamed up the safety razor in 1895. The first versions were on sale by 1901. The metal blade soon blunted, making it the definitive factory-made 'throwaway' item.

28

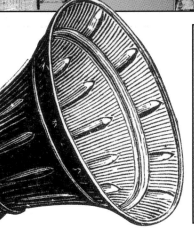

The vacuum flask was invented by Scot James Dewar (1842–1923) in 1885. Used in laboratories to keep liquids hot or cold, heat could not cross the vacuum gap. In the 1900s mass produced versions were used for hot drinks.

Inside a vacuum flask

Stopper

Outer case

Inner glass case

Vacuum between silvered walls of inner and outer case

Drink

COLOURS

In 1900 colour photography was possible but very expensive and complicated. The Lumière brothers (see page 13) turned their attention from cinema to colour photographs. They went back to the simple science of how different colours of light can be separated by filters. Their 1904 system was known as the autochrome method (below). It gave the pictures an extra-bright 'spotty' quality similar to the type of painting known as Impressionism which was popular at the time. In 1907 the Lumières set up in business with the world's first practical colour photography system.

A 1919 autochrome photo, Old Familiar Flowers.

THE AUTOCHROME PROCESS

This method used a flat plate, coated with tiny grains of potato starch. The grains were in layers dyed three colours, violet and green and orange, to act as colour filters. The green grains absorbed all colours of light except green, which they let through, and so on. (A similar system today is used for television screens where three colours, red and green and blue, combine to make all other colours.) The different colours of light hit the light-sensitive emulsion layer. When viewed through the layers they tinted different parts of the picture their different colours.

1 Glass plate or flexible film coated with adhesive

2 Dyed transparent potato starch grains added as colour filters

3 Varnish and light-sensitive layer of emulsion added

29

GLOSSARY

AMMONIA A chemical substance containing nitrogen and hydrogen, chemical formula NH_3. In pure form it is a choking, poisonous, yellowish gas. It is a basic substance for the chemical industry, especially for making nitrogen-rich substances such as nitric acid and artificial fertilizers, used in agriculture.

ASSEMBLY LINE A continuous series of machines and workers along which a product passes during its manufacture.

ATOM The smallest part of a pure substance (chemical element) that can exist naturally. Most atoms are made of three types of even tinier particles called protons, neutrons and electrons.

ELECTROMAGNETIC SPECTRUM A whole range or spectrum of waves consisting of combined electrical and magnetic energy. They include radio and TV waves, microwaves, infra-red, light rays, ultra-violet, X-rays and gamma rays.

INTERNAL COMBUSTION ENGINE An engine where the fuel is burned or combusted inside a contained place, usually a cylinder, as found in a petrol or diesel engine.

MASS PRODUCTION The manufacture of products which are standard or all much the same, in very large quantities, usually by machines and assembly lines.

PETROLEUM Crude oil, the usually thick, dark substance from under the ground, which is the basis of the oil or petrochemical industries.

RELATIVITY A set of scientific ideas which says that every quantity is variable and relative to everything else, including distance, movement, mass and time. The only constant quantity is the speed of light.

TURBINE A motor or device with angled blades fixed to a rotating central shaft, like a spinning fan.

VALVE An electronic device which looks like a small glass tube with metal parts (electrodes) inside. Valves have various jobs, such as using a very small, varying electric current to control a much larger current.

X-RAYS Types of electro-magnetic waves where the waves are very short (millions in one millimetre).

WORLD EVENTS

- •Boxer Rising in China
- •UK Labour Party begins
- •Queen Victoria of Great Britain dies
- •Second Boer War ends in South Africa
- •Canada and US settle dispute over Alaska
- •Japan at war with Russia (to 1905)
- •First phase of Russian Revolution
- •San Francisco earthquake in US
- •New Zealand acquires Dominion status
- •Austria annexes Bosnia-Herzegovina
- •Young Turks overthrow Sultan
- •Union of South Africa created
- •Chinese revolution: emperor overthrown
- •Balkan Wars (to '13)
- •King George of Greece assassinated
- •Outbreak of World War I
- •ANZAC troops slaughtered on Gallipoli
- •Ireland: Easter Rising in Dublin
- •Russian Revolution
- •US enters war
- •World War I ends
- •UK: women get vote
- •Treaty of Versailles
- •Nazi Party founded

TIMELINE

	SCIENCE EVENTS	TECHNOLOGY	FAMOUS SCIENTISTS	INVENTIONS
00	•Hugo de Vries works out genetic principles	•Benjamin Holt begins work on caterpillar tracks	•Friedrich Dorn discovers the rare gas radon	•First vacuum cleaner patented by Hubert Booth
01	•First Nobel Prizes awarded	•Marconi sends radio signals across the Atlantic	•Ferdinand Braun builds a simple crystal-radio set	•Mercury vapour arc lamp (early fluorescent tube)
02	•'Neanderthal Man' reconstructed from fossils	•Robert Bosch puts spark plugs in petrol engines	•Pavlov's conditioning experiments with dogs	•Willis Carrier devises an air conditioner machine
03	•Wright brothers' first powered flight	•Einthoven makes a medical ECG machine	•Ernest Rutherford names gamma rays	•Siemens builds an electric railway locomotive
04	•Bjerknes' first scientific weather forecasts	•Autochrome colour films patented by Lumière brothers	•George Hale sets up Mt Wilson Observatory	•Ludwig's photo-electric cell (electricity from light)
05	•Einstein's Special Theory of Relativity	•First U-boat submarine launched	•Alfred Binet devises the 'IQ' intelligence test	•Surgeon J Murphy's first artificial hip joint
06	•Earthquake evidence shows Earth has a core	•Voice and music broadcast by radio	•Marie Curie is Sorbonne's first woman professor	•Light bulbs with tungsten filaments
07	•Ytterbium first named, after a Swedish village	•Paul Cornu's first helicopter flight	•William Thomson, Baron Kelvin, dies	•First experiments with synthetic plastic, Bakelite
08	•Tyrannosaurus fossils first found in Montana	•First steel toothed bits to drill into rock for oil	•Hans Geiger devises a radiation detector (counter)	•Model T Ford launched •Cellophane developed
09	•Louis Blériot flies across the Channel	•S P L Sorensen begins use of pH scale for acidity	•Mohorovicic discovers the 'moho' layer in the Earth	•Enrico Forlanini tests first successful hydrofoil
0	•Ehrlich's first 'magic bullet' drug, salvarsan	•Charles Steinmetz warns of power station pollution	•Marie Curie produces pure form of radium	•First seaplane flown
1	•First Solvay Meeting for study of the atom	•Escalators on the London Underground	•Rutherford's 'solar system' idea of the atom	•First motorized washing machine
2	•The name 'vitamin' for healthy food is invented	•First tests to prove the existence of cosmic rays	•Bragg, father and son, measure X-ray wavelength	•Duralumin & stainless steel developed
3	•Bohr proposes shell idea for atomic structure	•Vacuum triode valves for long-distance phone calls	•Charles Fabry discovers ozone layer in atmosphere	•First geothermal power station opens, in Italy
4	•Rutherford discovers the proton	•First hi-tech sewage plant in Manchester, England	•Robert Goddard begins experiments with rockets	•Traffic lights first installed, in US
5	•Einstein's General theory of relativity	•First telephone call by radio across the Atlantic	•Blacksmith A Fruehauf makes trailers for tractors	•Chemical weapons first used in warfare
6	•'Barnard' stars seen by Edward Barnard	•Kotaro Honda devises early super-magnet alloys	•Scientist Ernst Mach dies	•Tanks first used in battle including Little Willie
7	•Early predictions of the existence of black holes	•First purpose-designed bomber plane, the Gotha	•Hale's 2.5-metre telescope installed on Mt Wilson	•Clarence Birdseye starts deep-freezing food
8	•Planck's Nobel Prize for quantum theory	•First radio link between England and Australia	•Francis Aston builds first mass spectrograph machine	•Alexander Graham Bell greatly improves hydrofoil
9	•Eclipse observations support relativity theory	•Ernest Rutherford reports on splitting the atom	•Karl von Frisch discovers 'waggle dance' of bees	•Daily air flights between Paris and London

INDEX